THE MAGNIFICENT MUSINGS OF McNICKLE

HUMOROUS THOUGHTS ON HUMOROUS THINGS

THE MAGNIFICENT MUSINGS OF McNICKLE

HUMOROUS THOUGHTS ON HUMOROUS THINGS

BY

McNICKLE

ILLUSTRATIONS BY MICHAEL DIEDERICH

www.magnificentmusings.net

The characters and events in this book are fictitious, except many that aren't.

"The Five Main Food Groups" is a revised version of an article that appeared in The Wilton Bulletin in 2004 with a different title.

Legal note: An improperly pickled pickle can breed botulism and lead to death by pickle.

Dedication

Dedicated to my Mother, out of general and specific gratitude, and to Vicky, without whose enthusiasm this book may not exist, so you can blame her.

Special thanks to Rebecca Patterson for her sublime encouragement (and for her enchanting parrot, which looks like a painting but seems alive to me).

With endless appreciation to Paul Levin for his trademark kindness and care.

Incredible thanks to Michael Diederich for his illustrious illustrations, artistry and humor.

And huge thanks to all my family...

Contents

Roundhouse of Worship   1

Disappointing Geographical Nomenclature   4

If I Had Been Abraham Lincoln   8

The Five Basic Food Groups   13

Leo's Line   17

History Unhidden   22

Possible Snakicide   25

A Rhodes More Traveled   30

Unnatural Selection   37

The Sound of Music – Working Song Titles   40

Pickle In Peace   44

Letter to the Pope   47

Randos   49

Texas Governor's Declaration of Independence   53

The Quick Brown Fox   57

New Curse Word   61

If A Bear Attacks Play Dead?   63

Dietary Restrictions   66

Guns for God   68

Screen Speeches On The Cutting Room Floor   73

I Don't Like Killing Frogs   76

If A Tree Falls In The Forest   78

A "Bro" Breaks Up   80

Severe Tire Damage   83

You Can Keep The Old West   86

The Secret Life of Bob Mitty   89

Averting Unmuting Disaster   93

The Lazy Dog   96

Disappointing Geographical Nomenclature Part 2   101

History Unhidden II   105

THE MAGNIFICENT MUSINGS OF McNICKLE

HUMOROUS THOUGHTS ON HUMOROUS THINGS

Roundhouse of Worship

The movie *Wonder Woman* is something I enjoyed.

I really liked the World War I angle. I also saw something in that movie I've never seen before. Never thought of. Surprised they thought of it.

I'm talking about when Wonder Woman punches a church. I didn't see it coming. Neither did the church. And though I've never seen anyone punch a church before, I doubt there's much room for improvement in Wonder Woman's church-punching. She punched that church right in the tower and it went down. Not a complete collapse, but there won't be services this Sunday.

I didn't see any churches on that cloudy island Wonder Woman is from, so I wonder if it was her first church-punch?

Someone who gets in a lot of fights with churches would probably nail their church-punch, but I don't know if it's automatic for a first-time holy house hitter to knock out an edifice.

I researched church-punching. Found nothing. Still I was curious, how did Wonder Woman become a church-puncher?

Maybe she started on a shed. Either it went well or she had to take out several sheds until she got shed-punching right and took on a shack. Maybe she dropped the shack with a single punch. Possibly with a kick to finish it off. Then perhaps she punched a detached garage to prepare for punching a cottage, then maybe a house and possibly a mansion and probably a commercial building or two before she punched a chapel, which I'm guessing is the last step on the path to punching a church.

But if Wonder Woman started as a shed-puncher and worked her way up, I think we would've heard about it. Maybe not shed-punching, but I think garage-punching would cause a stir, let alone cottage- or chapel-punching.

And if someone else had punched a church before Wonder Woman punched her church, I think we would've heard about that too.

Which leads me to believe that the church Wonder Woman punched might be the first church ever punched.

Not the kind of thing you root for but impressive when you see it.

Disappointing Geographical Nomenclature

I like mountains. For me, mountains are excellent.

As for mountain names, I like Everest. I like the name Kilimanjaro even better.

To me, many mountains have good or at least fully acceptable names. Chomo Yummo, Denali and Matterhorn are all nicely named. Whatever a matter is, this one has a horn. (Turns out Matter is a Swiss valley. They should sell t-shirts that say "What's the Matter?")

Ararat (Turkey) is nice. I don't think anyone could criticize Lamlam (Guam). One of my favorite mountain names is Annapurna (Nepal). I also like Masherbrum

(Pakistan) and Benbulben (Ireland). Jungfrau (Switzerland) is fun to say. As are Marmolejo, Chumpe and Uturunku, all in the Andes.

As far as I'm concerned, most mountains are fairly well-named. Which brings us to an exception. A huge exception (literally). I'm talking about the world's second-highest mountain: K-2.

Is that not a disappointing name, especially for such a prominent protrusion? I can see how the m.n.'s (the mountain namers) might toy with the digit 2 here, but coupling it with K goes nowhere for me. How about something catchy, like Mt. Uppahiya?

I almost looked into how Mt. K-2 got its name, but what's done is done. All I know is I could've done better.

P.S. I just looked into it. The name is from a geographical survey conducted in 1856 and was meant to be a temporary designation until the local name could be determined, which is how the m.n.'s normally do it.

The K is for Karakorum, the mountain range it's in, and the 2 is because it's the second peak the surveyors saw in the range. The mountain they designated K-1 turned out to have a local name of Masherbrum, which seems fitting. Whatever a masher is, this one has a brum. (Turns out brum means mountain, but there's dispute over what masher means.) And I already coincidentally like that mountain name, so it feels like we're friends.

But for K-2 the surveyors could never find a local name, even after asking around quite a bit. Since the mountain couldn't be seen from any villages and the surveyors were unable to discover a name, they concluded it didn't have a name and it's because it had never been seen.

Which might seem surprising, because if you head up the Baltoro Glacier, go past Masherbrum and turn left at the next glacier, K-2 is right ahead, rising alone from the ice. You can't miss it. It's tall.

Yet without a warm jacket, serious boots, crampons and climbing rope there's no way to head up the Baltoro Glacier. Or a reason to. If you lived close enough back then to potentially hike up the Baltoro Glacier, you're already in a harsh high-altitude world of wrinkles and death with mountains all around, why take more risk to see more big icy lumps you can't climb and are thrilled not to?

I'm guessing someone saw K-2 before 1856, but it would've meant traversing an extremely treacherous glacier with very primitive equipment just to have a look around. They didn't know the world's second-highest mountain was back there. So they would've been adding more danger to their already dangerous lives just to see more scenery like the scenery they already saw all day. What would be the point? Maybe 1856 is the first time it was ever seen. I'm guessing we'll never know.

Since K-2 was never meant to be a permanent name, as far I'm concerned the mountain has never been named. So I'm starting a movement to name it.

I propose calling it "Viśvāusa Garna Sakdina Whamaki'iṁ Yuham̊ Sabai Sajai Sṅgai Chu!"

It means "I Can't Believe You Didn't Know About Me, I've Been Here All Along!"

If I Had Been Abraham Lincoln

It's probably good that I wasn't Abraham Lincoln.

I would've wanted to end slavery just as much as he did, but I don't think I would've handled it the same way.

If the South had said to me "Hey North," because that's the nickname they would've had for me, "we're sick of you telling us what to do. We're leavin' and you can't stop us!" as much as I would've wanted to get rid of slavery and save the Union, I don't think it would've occurred to me to do what Abe did, let alone try it.

Instead of saying sayonara—and Abe was fluent in Japanese so he could've—Abe basically said: "South, this is a union and you can't break it. So if you leave we're going to kill you and keep killing you until you come back!"

It worked, aside from 618,000 dead soldiers, but I probably would've said something like "South, I am crestfallen. Dolorous. Yet I know it's a big decision for you, so... I won't stand in your way. Good luck!"

"You're okay if we go??"

"I am gutted, but you do you."

"We don't have to fight?'

"If you love something set it free. If it loves you it will come back. Someone should write a book about that concept."

"Shouldn't we at least negotiate about us maybe staying?"

"I think a clean break is probably best. Well, great seeing you!"

It's awkward. South heads off.

"South, wait up."

South turns hopefully. "Yes??"

"You think Texas might want to go with you? If you want to ask... up to you. Hey, do you need any help packing? Oh right, you're just leaving politically. And you can have Fort Sumter. We can be out tonight."

That's probably about what I would've said. I think I would've expected South to come crawling back. Even if Congress had decided to go to war I still would've expected it to go something like this, in which I, as Abe, nicknamed North, refer to myself in the third person...

It's August, 1863, six weeks after Gettysburg. North is in a bar in Boston having a good time. Things are looking up, though why Meade didn't pursue Lee still rankles. North sips from a beer that isn't Samuel Adams because it hasn't been invented yet and sees South entering the bar.

South spots North. "North! What are you doing here?"

"It's my local when I'm in town. What are you doing here??"

"Me? I just happened to be in the area and got a whale of a thirst. I had no idea you'd be here. Total coincidence."

South notices an African-American man in the bar.

"Whoa! Escaped slave. Get him!"

"No, South! He's an employee. Sit down!"

"Sorry, instinct. When you say 'employee,' you don't mean they pay him, do you? They just give him bed and food and charge him more than he makes, right?"

North: "LaMarcus is the manager. He's paid well and he deserves it."

South: "But he's paid less than people who are… pallid?"

North: "He makes an excellent salary plus tips and I happen to know they pay into a retirement fund for him here. Any tavern in town would take him."

South: "I have major misgivings about that business model but potato-potahto. Hey, I just thought of something since we're both here, totally randomly in my case. Do you want to have a beer and see if we can't settle our differences? Put this little ol' war behind us."

North signals LaMarcus, who brings two beers. North gives South a look. South realizes he's supposed to tip. South puts a coin on the table. North holds the look. South adds a coin.

"So, South, you want to rejoin the country?"

"Very much! I mean, we're open to discussion."

"You can come back, South, no problem."

"Seriously? Oh, thank you!"

"But we're getting rid of the Electoral College."

"No! Never. You can't tell us what to do—actually, I don't want Montana to have all that power if they ever become a state. Okay, no electoral college. Great, we're done! See you under the rotunda—"

"You know there's something else."

"Let me guess: you wanna talk about that Proclamation thingy."

"I do."

"Here's another guess: you want us to get rid of our slaves."

"You're a good guesser."

"How about we free all our slaves except for some?"

"Either free all the slaves or don't come back."

"Fine, we'll have different areas for white and... off white. Separate, but totally totally equal."

"No! And I'm outlawing white sheets! From now on all white sheets are illegal."

"Why??"

"Just a hunch."

The Five Basic Food Groups

For several years I lived in Connecticut, about 50 miles from Manhattan. A version of this was published in 2004 in what historians refer to as a "newspaper."

We who are lucky enough to live in Wilton usually live here for a reason: the abundance of nature, both floral and faunal. If I were to coin a motto for this magical town it would be: *Where The City Ends and The Country Begins.* (Note: If the town wants to pay me some coin for my motto I'm open.)

Having two-acre zoning and numerous large tracts of municipal forest make Wilton a bucolic Eden, made even more special by its proximity to the city. Yet recently I learned there's another side to nature's glory here.

The house I live in, on almost ten wooded acres next to more wooded acres, has an attached workshop/shed accessible from the garage and the outside. For years a humble groundhog made its home beneath the shed. (Actually, I have no idea if the groundhog was humble. Groundhogs in general seem humble, but as groundhogs go maybe this one was cocky.) Occasionally I would see it going in and out of its little opening under the shed, but unless cornered a groundhog is docile and I'm not a cornerer of wild animals, so we coexisted like religions on a bumpersticker.

I left the house for several months, returning in January. Once most of the snow melted I noticed the groundhog house's opening was quite a bit bigger, yet I innocently thought maybe she or he just had a lot of friends over and needed better access. I'd seen tracks in the snow of another type of animal, but I didn't realize the groundhog might not be living under the shed anymore. I soon found out it definitely wasn't.

One day in late winter I entered the shed from the garage and started to exit onto the patio when my friend, who was in the house by a sliding glass door, shouted "Look, there's a fox!" I looked out the shed door and saw on the patio an extremely wide fox trying to hurry away, but I didn't make the connection that my presence in the shed had roused the corpulent canid.

About five weeks later I drove into the long driveway and there, alone, with a winsomely endearing face and a head way too big for its body, was the cutest little baby fox I've ever seen. I've actually never seen any other baby foxes, I just didn't know how to end that sentence, but the fox's size and especially its face were insanely cute, backed by an expression of love and curiosity. An oven mitt with legs and a smile.

The little thing didn't move, it just stared at me. I decided to leave the car in the driveway and got out and stood there. The baby fox was looking at me almost as if it wanted to be petted. I wanted to pet it, but I wasn't thinking seriously along those lines, though 25% of me was. (Maybe 41%.) We made significant eye contact then it wobbled away. Turns out it was just learning to walk.

The next day I saw the little thing on a small rise about 50 feet away, alone, staring at me, same expression. Over the next two days I saw it several times, walking better, always by itself and staring at me. The tiny tyke seemed to be alone quite a bit for something that young and small, and I began to wonder if something had happened to its parents and it was staring at me out of need.

I've only lived in Wilton a few years, so I asked people who've been here a long time if they thought a baby fox would act that way normally or only if it were an orphan, and everyone thought it was probably normal.

But the question still lingered: was the baby fox alone and hungry?

I went outside near the shed for the first time in a week yesterday and the question was definitively answered. No baby fox could leave what I saw. Few bears could leave what I saw.

Outside the den I saw: a squirrel tail, part of a raccoon pelt, skunk fur, sections of a rabbit, unidentified gnawed bones, a severed but undamaged Canada goose head, two disconnected goose feet, a doggy chew toy (!) and the carcass of a large bird that was probably the goose but could've been a turkey.

I'm relieved the baby fox is being provided for, but I wish the foxes would move out. Yet why would they? The woods are basically a supermarket of mammal meat, what would make them go?

Note: that last question isn't rhetorical. What would make them go?

LEO'S LINE

"Happy families are all alike; every unhappy family is unhappy in its own way."

That's the famous first line of Leo Tolstoy's classic 1878 novel *Anna Karenina*, a first line that's a long way from the last line.

I hate to quibble with Leo, and I get the part about unhappiness being different in every unhappy family, but are happy families really all alike?

It's a beloved sentiment, which is why I've never said anything, but does the happy-families-are-all-alike thesis hold up to rigorous academic scrutiny? We'll never know because all I can apply is haphazard minor speculation, but that won't stop me.

I've seen happy families. Some are rigid and strict. Some are bohemian and loose. Others just have money. Or really cool cars. Or really cool cars and money. Or really cool cars and money and a dynamic social life. Maybe a second home.

I know fun happy families. I know boring happy families. (Seems like a lot of happy families are boring, and a lot of boring families are happy. There are advantages to not dabbling in excitement.)

It's a snappy statement by Leo, but after 146 years I think it's time to say it: happy families are not all alike. I actually think it would be hard to find two.

Since the doubter of a famous phrase must be thorough, I made a list of different types of happy families to make sure I wasn't out of line. I don't mean to rub it in, but I came up with 63 different types.

It's pretty easy.

Here's ten:

<u>Types of Happy Families (partial list)</u>:

Those who know they are happy.

Those who don't know they are happy but are.

Those who believe they are happy but aren't sure, but are.

Those who hope they are happy but are too timid to dig deeper and would probably be much happier if they did dig deeper, yet are happy, though barely.

Those who think they are happy but aren't, yet they're so convinced they're happy what's the difference? (It's best to avoid these families.)

Those who are happy but have doubts, yet they're going through a transition period so they'll be fine.

A family with four who are happy, a fifth who jumps in and out of happiness like a valence electron, and a sixth who's capable of making several people unhappy at any moment, but the last person is getting help and showing real progress, is happy, but it's different from a happy family with six kids and twelve off-road vehicles and they live in the desert and ride everyday and all the kids get good grades.

I'm surprised Leo couldn't see the difference between a now-happy family who used to live next door to a complete a******, then moved to a lovely cul-de-sac with a friendly social scene and is forever appreciative, and a happy family of boaters who boat a lot and have always boated.

That's ten types of happy families. Let me know if you'd like the other 53.

I looked into Leo. His story is interesting if you like hearing about things you're glad you didn't do. As a child of Russian nobility his parents weren't around much, especially after they died when he was young, and as an adult he was legendarily bothered by not knowing the purpose of life, which makes me think the idea of a happy family was so foreign to his own experience that happy families all looked alike to him much like cheetahs all look alike to me, yet to another cheetah some are real lookers.

Leo was born rich and got richer through writing, yet he never really found a basket for his spiritual eggs. He tried drinking, sex and religion, all with great gusto and regrettable results, and later got into quite a few fights with his wife because he thought they should give away all their money and live like peasants, which unsettles a spouse. (She fought for and got some of his copyrights. Good for her, he wasn't using them.)

Nothing really made Leo happy the way he hoped, but in addition to the renowned novels (*War and Peace*) he wrote a lot of important social and political stuff, including a famous 1908 published letter arguing that nonviolent resistance would be India's best path to freedom. This was 39 years before India gained independence and before nonviolence was really a thing. The letter inspired Gandhi, then a lawyer in South Africa, who requested proof that the letter was written by the celebrated author, which Tolstoy provided and they became friends. (A four-hundred-page letter would've been proof enough for me.)

Anyway, happy families are not all alike, but tall families are.

History Unhidden
Little-Known Facts About Historical Figures

Joan of Arc didn't actually live in Arc, but kept a small apartment there.

John James Audubon fell in love with a hooded merganser.

Hannibal first tried to cross the Alps with hippos.

In addition to writing the poem *The Divine Comedy*, Dante wrote limericks. Scholars believe this one is autobiographical:

There once was a poet from Italy
who arranged his words so prettily
but when talkin' to women
his words weren't so swimmin'
and he has yet to engage his virility

The Dalai Lama wears Mormon undergarments. "They just fit right. I'm high-waisted."

More than an apple fell on Newton's head. There was also a dead bird, some loose bark and quite a bit of hail.

Napoleon was known to wait three weeks before opening his mail, figuring by then most urgent matters would be resolved. This led to the foreclosure of all his storage units.

Fidel Castro secretly invested his retirement money with Warren Buffett.

American independence activist Thomas Paine's famous pamphlet "Common Sense" was originally titled "Biteth Me, King George."

Vacuum designer James Dyson's first venture was a fan, then he realized suction pays more.

Charles Darwin's groundbreaking book *On The Origin of Species* was originally titled *On The Female Of Species*, and was entirely sketches of nude women, then someone noticed the animal stuff.

Possible Snakicide

Watching a baseball game on tv once I thought I killed my friend's snake.

I was at Eric's house to watch the Anaheim Angels playoff game then the St. Louis Cardinals playoff game.

I was sitting in Eric's nice maroon leather chair with the Angels holding a one-run lead and me holding a corn snake, while for some reason Angels manager Mike Scioscia didn't put in relief pitcher Troy Percival for three consecutive Yankees, including Bernie Williams, who hit a three-run homer, when the snake slid from my fingers down past the seat cushion into the cavity of the chair. I wasn't concerned at first, but Eric didn't take the news well at all. Worse than the three-run homer.

The four-foot snake, which was pretty when the light hit it, was now in the dark, sealed inside a fabric chair bottom. Eric thought the snake would never come out and would die in there, or it would come out in a week or two and escape outdoors. Eric's wife, Vicky, agreed and said it would probably get eaten by the owl that hangs around their house in the hills.

We turned the chair over carefully, and as I was prying off premium-quality upholstery staples with a tiny-handled screwdriver and inadequate pliers (musicians aren't known for their toolkits), Vicky heard a noise outside, where we went and she shined a flashlight on an owl the size of a fire hydrant. I think it was salivating.

I went back inside and turned the attention of my little-screwdriver-that-could to the chair's grapefruit-sized wooden feet, which were attached with extra-long wood screws that take extra-long to unscrew, especially when you're being glared at by you-know-who.

When I finally got two of the feet off, the bottom fabric was loose at a corner and I could peek inside the chair. It was dark but I saw blood all over! Purple-reddish blood. I announced with sadness and a brief contemplation and dismissal of guilt that there was blood in the chair. The Angels had lost their lead in the 8th and now Eric's snake was trapped and bleeding inside his favorite piece of furniture, which was partially dismantled and smeared in blood. Eric was not happy. Neither I guessed was the snake.

Despite his normal sunny open breeziness, if confronted with trouble you know when Eric is bothered. He tells you. "You *should* feel bad that the snake got in there! I assumed when you asked to hold it that you knew what you were doing" he charmingly shouted. I choked off a factual retort along the lines of "It was your idea for me to hold it" and said "How much is a corn snake?" These words did not console Eric, though Vicky was like "You don't have to get a new one, let it die." Accountants can be that way, though it wasn't exactly a charismatic snake.

Unfortunately the undynamic serpent was beloved by their two young sons, meaning that news of the attractive snake's demise would bring down the curtain on the innocence phase of the boys' nascent lives and force them to face the fact that the world, especially their parents' snake-snuffing friend, is a terrible place.

All this was going through my mind as I showed Eric the blood. To my great relief he said "That's not blood."

It was maroon leather dye. Even with this news there was no joy in Eric's eyes.

Eventually I removed enough staples from the fabric on the bottom of the chair for Eric to shine a flashlight into the chair's intricate interior truss system, which offered several places for an ambitious snake to hide, and Eric yelled "I see it!" Grabbing his youngest son's mini Dodgers bat and exhorting me to hold the flashlight, Eric tried to pull the snake out, but the tiny bat was too short for the snake's determination, so Eric got his older son's 3-foot plastic grim reaper pole—which I hope is from a Halloween costume and not a prop in some twisted ritual involving incense and entrails—and, wearing an oven mitt the size of an arm pad worn by people who train German attack dogs, he lifted the snake out of the chair and carried it back to its terrarium down the hall, while simultaneously suggesting that I should probably never touch a snake again, and if for some reason I did I should be much more careful around first-class furniture (though how classy can it be if the inside leather dye looks like it was applied by monkeys with a liquor problem?).

Fortunately the Cardinals trounced the Diamondbacks and the owl went hungry.

And the Angels won the World Series.

P.S. Eric never offered me an oven mitt!

A Rhodes More Traveled

Recently, descendants of Civil War soldier Elisha Hunt Rhodes found an antique trunk that was hidden away in an attic. Inside the trunk was a dusty bundle of old letters.

The family was thrilled to find the letters. Now that Elisha Hunt Rhodes is famous for his letters and journals used by director Ken Burns in the landmark documentary "The Civil War," more letters from Elisha would be quite a find, both historically and financially.

Elisha Hunt Rhodes was a Union Army success story, rising from corporal to colonel, and an eloquent explainer of a soldier's life, who also had success after the war in business and politics. Someone to admire.

So when the descendants saw the initials E.H.R. above the return address on all the envelopes they were jubilant. More letters from Elisha!

Then they noticed the letters weren't from Elisha, they were to Elisha. Turns out they were from his brother, Ethan Hunt Rhodes, an ancestor the family had never heard of. The family was even more jubilant. Letters from one pillar of valor to his virtuous brother would be even more important and more valuable and bring even more honor to the Rhodes family!

Then they read the letters.

<u>Letter #1</u>:

"May 30, 1862

Dear Elisha, we are bivouacked by the Chickahominy River! At least I think we're bivouacked. Maybe we're just camped, I forget the difference. Brother, I know the country is divided and we need to stop slavery, but this war crap is terrible. I don't want to get shot and I don't want to shoot! And I don't want to stab neither. I'd rather shoot than stab, but it takes so long to reload that sometimes stabbing is the only way. To me that should be a warning sign about the whole endeavor!"

Letter #2:

"Dear Elisha, I met a girl. She dressed well but undressed even better. I tell you, brother, seeing her in the morning light was like getting a free meal the day after a battle in which you don't lose your leg.

Then I met the girl's father. We weren't formally introduced. He found us in the barn and jumped to a lot of conclusions. Mostly correct conclusions. As I write this I am in the medical tent getting buckshot picked out of my behind."

Letter #3:

"Met my first people of African heritage today. It did not go well. They were great but I tried so hard to show I wasn't racist that I think I seemed racist."

Letter #4:

"Aunt Eunice keeps writing about the great letters you always send. Elisha, Elisha, Elisha. That's all I hear. You were always better at bat-balls and hoop rolling and now this!"

Letter #5:

"This morning I missed the battle! I set my alarm for 6, but it was 6pm, not 6am. I could've kicked myself! Half the regiment died so at least I'm still alive, but I'm pretty chagrinned. I'm also in the stockade, where I'll be for the next three months."

Letter #6:

"I'm thinking of heading to Canada. It's not just the war. Going to the doctor is free. And Canadians are so polite. The only downside is they expect you to be just as polite. It's exhausting!"

Letter #7:

"I deserted! It's way too dangerous being a soldier, especially those battles. It's a great cause, don't get me wrong, but I'm hoping to contribute from off the battlefield. I think I can do it from Brazil. I'm already here so I think I should try. I know, I can send a monthly newsletter of battle tips and plantain recipes! *Keep your head down and the flame low,* stuff like that."

Letter #8:

"The women in Brazil wear so much less clothing. The other day I saw an ankle! It is wanton down here!"

Letter #9:

"I'm in Rio de Janeiro. They wear big things on their heads and dance in the street here. It looks like fun so I'm trying to find plumes. They're like feathers with attitude.

They have an amazing mountain overlooking the city. They should put a huge statue up there! I'm thinking something in a nude."

Letter #10:

"The long arm of the Union Army finally caught me! I was captured bodysurfing in a speedo off Copacabana Beach and put on a ship to be taken home and court-martialed. It's a shame I won't get to samba anymore. I trained each hip to have a mind of its own!

Note: A speedo is a rather brief costume for swimming. Maybe someday they won't be made of wool so my personal harbor doesn't get so itchy."

Letter #11:

"I taught the sailors to samba. We're putting on a shipboard show tonight!"

Letter #12:

"I escaped! I'm on a clipper ship bound for Suriname.

By the way, how is Sherman's march to the sea going? It's a shame he'll be there in late fall/early winter. The shore is so cold then. It's still worth going but nothing like summer. And Atlanta will be left alone, right?"

"I'm in big trouble. Never made it to Suriname. I was hijacked up the Amazon and now I'm a slave to an indigenous tribe that wears no clothing and hunts with blowdarts!

The nudity is nice but all day I'm making blowdarts. I'm getting really good at it but being a slave sucks. Yet I'm just one person. How can I fight back? I wish someone would fight for me. Stand up for my rights! Oh, that's what I was doing in the Union Army. Wow, irony."

That was the last letter, found three years later in a bottle that washed up near Manaus.

According to a note local missionaries inserted in the envelope after the letter was found, Ethan escaped around the date of the letter.

No one knows what he did after that, but there are several extremely remote tribes with people who look surprisingly like him, so we have a pretty good idea.

Un-Natural Selection

The Copenhagen Zoo was in the news not long ago for two animal incidents.

First they euthanized a healthy giraffe, then a month later they killed four thriving lions. The zoo said the giraffe was at risk for inbreeding and the lions were likely to be killed by a new dominant male.

For educational reasons the giraffe was dismembered in front of visitors, including children as young as four, then fed to lions, probably some of the same lions killed a month later. (At least the lions got a home meal before their slaughter.)

Luckily I was in Denmark that weekend so I investigated. I dug in a dumpster behind the zoo and found the minutes from a recent board meeting.

Most of the minutes were covered in lion blood, but I was able to find a clean fragment and have it translated.

ZOO PRESIDENT: ...so it's agreed, we expand the monkey cages. Excellent! Now let's talk about acquiring new animals. I was thinking we could get a snow leopard. They have such cool paws. Who wants to get a snow leopard?

Everyone excitedly raises their hand.

ZOO PRESIDENT: Okay, we get a snow leopard for the Copenhagen Zoo! Wonderful. Now what are we thinking we do with it?

VICE PRESIDENT OF DESIGN: We could build a natural habitat! I am a wizard with artificial rock.

ZOO PRESIDENT: You do put the art in artificial, but I had another idea. What if we kill it?

EVERYONE: Yes, excellent! Kill it!

ZOO PRESIDENT: Okay, we get a snow leopard, then kill it. What else should we get?

VICE PRESIDENT OF REPTILES: How about a Komodo dragon?! Who doesn't like a giant lizard that eats people??

ZOO PRESIDENT: Done! But part of my job is taking the temperature of a room, and my inner thermometer tells me this room is of one mind: let's kill the Komodo!

EVERYONE: Yes! In front of toddlers!

VICE PRESIDENT OF MOATS AROUND CAGES: Instead of having visitors watch us kill the Komodo, or any perfectly healthy animal we arbitrarily choose to terminate, what if we let the visitors do the killing??

VICE PRESIDENT OF MARKETING: We can offer different methods of death! For a thousand euro you get one shot to pop a dingo with a pistol from a distance, or for ten thousand you can go in-cage to heave a harpoon!

ZOO PRESIDENT: Excellent! Great morning, everyone. Let's order lunch. What would you like?

EVERYONE: Vegan! Strictly vegan. Eating animals is unethical!

"The Sound of Music"
Working Song Titles

The movie *The Sound of Music* has it all: great story with real stakes, killer songs, incredible scenery, excellent acting and masterful direction.

Not to mention outstanding work by the key grip.

Most good musicals have one to three stellar songs. Hopefully more but it doesn't happen often. *Chicago* has one. *Cats* two. *Phantom of the Opera* really only one.

The Sound of Music has nine great songs! Both music and lyrics. All with excellent titles:

Maria
Climb Ev'ry Mountain
Do-Re-Mi
Edelweiss
The Lonely Goatherd
My Favorite Things
Sixteen Going on Seventeen
So Long, Farewell
The Sound of Music

But few people know that for each song in the legendary Rogers and Hammerstein musical, there were multiple working titles before they settled on the ones we've come to know and love.

A few years ago I was in Austria and met a man in Salzburg who knew Rogers (Hammerstein repeatedly snubbed him) and was there during the filming.

The man said one night Rogers, hopped up on edelweiss, told him "all the dumb titles Hammerstein originally proposed for my beautiful music. Why do songs even need words? They get in the way of the humming!"

According to the venerable Salzburger, these were the working song titles (with the final titles):

Nun For Me
Sondra
Maria

Cross Every Creek
Ascend A Lot of Heights
Climb Every Mountain
Climb Ev'ry Mountain

Small White Flowers
Leontopodium Nivale
Alpine Groundcover
Edelweiss

The Solitary Bovid Wrangler
The Dirty Herdboy
The Lonely Goatherd

My Totally Best Stuff
The Only Song That Mentions Brown Paper Packages
My Favorite Things

Jailbait
I Am Sixteen And Ready For Action
Sixteen Going On Seventeen

Adios You Nazi Bastards
Goodbye, Eff You
So Long, Farewell

The Noise of Vocal, Instrumental, or Mechanical
Sounds Having Rhythm, Melody, or Harmony
Audible Notes
The Sound of Music

Pickle in Peace

I came upon some reassurance once that seemed unnecessary.

It was the headline for an article written by homemaking marvel Martha Stewart. It said "Don't Be Intimidated By Pickle-Making Procedures."

I don't mean to sound invincible, but I've never even been lightly cowed by a picklemaker's work, let alone intimidated. Bison, cleavage, how to pronounce the word "quay" all intimidate me, but the pickling thing just isn't a bother.

When I saw the headline, my first reaction was that pickling seems to involve little more than soaking and waiting, mainly just soaking and waiting.

Turns out there are a lot of steps to pickling, mostly in the soaking part. Actually they're all in the soaking part. The waiting is as easy as it sounds. But none of the steps seem even challenging, let alone intimidating.

I guess I dodged a big bullet in life, because I am gloriously free of intimidation by the procedures for making a pickle. Whew.

P.S. In case, like me sometimes, you could use a reminder, "quay" is pronounced "key." Crazy, huh? I'm thinking of starting a movement to change the pronunciation. Or the spelling. Either way.

According to Merriam-Webster, a quay is "a structure built parallel to the bank of a waterway for use as a landing place." I'm a big fan of Merriam-Webster, but does that really crystallize it for you? A structure can be anything from Lego to limestone and a lot more. When I think of a quay, and I try not to, I think of a wall in a harbor that's flat on top for unloading. I'm sensing it can be more than that, but what are the parameters?

Word origin of *quay* (Merriam-Webster):

> alteration of earlier *key*, from Middle English, from Middle French dialect (Picard) *kay*, probably of Celtic origin; akin to Breton *kae* hedge, enclosure; akin to Old English *hecg* hedge

I was with them until they said *kae* is akin to hedge. I don't see it. *Hecg* is akin to hedge, sure, but not *kae* (pronounced key).

It's almost as if they don't know why quay is pronounced key.

I actually wouldn't be surprised if, like me, they're not even sure what a quay is, let alone why it's pronounced incorrectly.

Letter to the Pope

Several years ago I wrote a letter to Pope Benedict. The other day, to my great disappointment, I found it in a drawer. I forgot to mail it!

No wonder I never heard back.

Dear Pope Benedict,

In a recent writing, you say you're against scientists manipulating human genes. You warn against the attempt to "modify the very grammar of life as planned and willed by God." But how do you know it's not God's will for a wild genius to give me an extra arm so I can eat breakfast while driving? Why would God make the genius if I can't have the arm?

Just how can you be sure it's not God's will for us to be able manipulate human genes so that someday there will only be attractive people? I realize it's not important to you since you swore off interpersonal interludes, but why mess with my earthly delights?

And what makes you so certain it's not God's will for us to be able to make half-people/half-dogs so we can lick wherever we want and still open a can of horsemeat?

The Bible doesn't mention DNA. No offense, but it seems beyond your bailiwick. I think your non-religious expertise lies in telling people the different ways there are not to have sex and how to be okay being poor.

If God made the people who gave us the Pontiac Aztec, how do you know he's against us having thirteen livers so we can drink like a Kennedy?

love,
McNickle

Randos

A horse is actually 15 horsepower. I think we're owed an explanation.

Mountain goats aren't goats. They're even not in the same genus.

Hyenas are classified in the cat family. I need to speak to Carl Linnaeus.

Eating is a hassle. The average person eats over 1,000 times a year. A python eats twice a year. I'd love to have a goat every six months and be done with it.

The motto for Reno, Nevada is "The Biggest Little City in the World." That's either the best bad motto or the worst good motto I've ever heard.

It would be fun if poets unionized. Publishers would try to crush them but poets would nail them with irony, so both sides would think they're winning. Poets would demand to be paid by the stanza, while publishers would argue it would lead to only epic poems being written, causing a dangerous dearth of limericks. Publishers would try to impose a minimum standard of at least 10% of a poem being understandable, but poets would threaten not to use punctuation, so publishers would cave, at least for this contract. A rift would develop between rhyming poets and prose poets, with rhymers demanding higher rates, claiming rhymes induce more felicity, while prosers would proffer that their poems pack more profundity since they're not subservient to euphony. Finally, after a marathon late-night session, publishers would agree to drop their push to require poets to wear berets in public, if poets would agree to wear them at book signings and occasionally smoke.

Robert Plant wrote the lyrics "If there's a bustle in your hedgerow, don't be alarmed now." I agree! One bustle isn't an issue. Two maybe, three for sure, but I can shrug off the lone bustle.

I was saddened by a National Park Service notice. It said "Do not touch or move dead rabbits." There goes my weekend! There are few things I love more than spending long Saturdays and Sundays looking for dead rabbits, hoping to touch them. Not so much move them, touching would be enough. But dead rabbits are incredibly hard to find. I've looked probably every other weekend for eight years and never even seen a wobbly one, let alone a dead one. What an achievement it would be to find my first dead rabbit! But I wouldn't move it. Touching would be plenty. Which got me to wondering what dead animal I might be tempted to move, not just touch. If I saw a dead chinchilla I'd google to see if anything could be made from one pelt, but if not I wouldn't move it, though I'd probably touch it, unless there were a notice not to. Yet I doubt I'll ever get the chance to touch (or move) an expired chinchilla. Chinchillas live high in the Andes Mountains, so I'll probably never even see a living one, let alone a touchable dead one. Thinking about chinchillas reminded me that guinea pigs also live in the Andes. I'm not interested in touching or moving dead guinea pigs, but I started thinking how insecure a guinea pig must feel when it encounters a chinchilla. Chinchillas are prized for having the thickest fur of any land mammal. Guinea pigs cost a nickel in the mall. I bet guinea pigs somehow sense that chinchillas are highly sought-after while guinea pigs are pursued only by predators. And third-graders. No one has a guinea pig coat. Switzerland treats guinea pigs properly. Since guinea pigs live in groups in the wild, in Switzerland it's illegal to have only one guinea pig. As soon as you hear that you figure there must be a service in Switzerland to rent a guinea pig if one of your two guinea pigs dies. And they do have that service. Female meerschweinchen are about $70 and males are about $60, half of which you get back when you return your rented rodent. Because if your guinea pig dies, you don't want to mourn it from prison.

TEXAS GOVERNOR'S DECLARATION OF INDEPENDENCE

From time to time, we tough-talkin' Texans like to tout our legal right to secede from the United States, a right which many believe is enshrined in our state constitution, and belief is more than plenty.

While our secession talk may have receded of late, like floods and swallows it always returns, so in the interest of saving time when our skedaddle threat pops up again, here is the Texas Declaration of Independence. This should cover it legally.

If it don't work my gun do.

Date: ____/____/____

When in the course of human events, it becomes necessary for one people to dissolve the political bands which have connected the coolest state in the country to a country that is being mean to it, we, instead of working from within the country as it was designed to work—though we're totally gung ho to be American if we stay—we who are maybe leaving thought the least we could do is tell you why we're leaving, if we leave, which we may not. But we might, so watch out!

Compilation of grievances that could be the reason for our possible departure:

<u>Taxing Rich People</u>. We don't want taxes raised on the rich. A lot of us are rich, or are hoping to be rich, or just like havin' rich people around, and raising taxes on the rich makes 'em grumpy. We don't do grumpy in Texas, so we're secedin' if you raise taxes on 3% of the country and lower them for the other 97%! What do you think, the rich can just fend for themselves? Don't forget that the rich are always looking out for the little people. That's what they do, look, look, look. We need to support their richness!

Oil. Lately oil's been gettin' about as much respect as a mullet at the opera. People talk about solar or wind power. We can get to those, but for now do we really want all the fossils in the ground to have died in vain? We need to honor their memory by digging them up and burning them!

Gun Laws. Needless. Pointless. No can do! (If I think I need a canon how do you know I don't?)

Hats. Our secession will be caused by something else, but let's be honest, much of the country laughs when we visit with our hats on, which we often wear indoors, partly because hats are cool, partly because if we take 'em off we'll have hat hair, and partly because our swagger droops without 'em, so when we secede we're passin' a law requiring every living citizen to wear a hat, and when we say "every living citizen" that obviously includes fetuses. There might be some installation issues at first with those fetusi, but nuthin' our deep love of science down here can't cure.

Homosexualities. The Bible supposedly frowns on it, but the Bible frowns on shellfish and I love crawdads, so if you want to get married fine by me as long as I don't have to kiss you.

Wimmin'. I know y'all think we think we have the best women on the planet here, and we do think that, but only 'cause it's true. This ain't actually a grievance, it's a brag. Damn straight! And I would know: I'm a woman. At least I was. Kidding! Still am.

That's it so far.

For us it all comes down to compatibility: we're not compatible with the Constitution, unless we want to be.

The Constitution oughta be like the Bible: let us interpret!

The Quick Brown Fox

There's a sentence many people know that uses every letter of the alphabet: "The quick brown fox jumps over the lazy dog."

I have questions about the fox.

For one, how quick is it? Is it like all foxes in the quickness department, which is quite quick, or is it quick even for a fox? And if it is extra quick, how did it get that way? Was it born to a long line of fleet foxes, or was it raised in an environment requiring special skills, for instance a place where eagles are trained to swoop down and grip foxes and carry them off, like Romania?

Also, did the indolent canine notice the vulpine vault, or was the passive pup unaware of the aerial endeavor?

Unfortunately the answers to these questions, and questions even more interesting, are unavailable, unless we happen to run into the fox and it magically speaks.

What is that heading our way? Is it a fox? It is! Looks like a brown one. Is it the jumper?? Too bad foxes can't speak.

Fox: I can speak. Either that or I'm animatronic.

Me: That's amazing! How is it possible?

Fox: I learned by watching soap operas through a window. I still can't believe Sharon and Rey broke up!

Me: So sad.

Fox : And yes, I'm the jumper.

Me: Great to meet you. Let me ask you, are you quick?

Fox: Quick in general or quick for a fox?

Me: For a fox.

Fox: I happen to be quick even for a fox. You'd be quick too if you lived under constant threat of attack from trained Romanian eagles!

Me: Copy that. I notice your fur is brown for winter. Which coat do you prefer, winter brown or summer red?

Fox: What are you, an artist??

Me: Just curious. I've always wondered about you. You're pretty famous.

Fox: Thanks. I guess I prefer red. For sure the vixens like it.

Me: What made you jump the dog?

Fox (unconvincing): I like to jump. All foxes do. We like the wind in our fur.

Me: That's it??

Fox (fesses up): Let's just say there's little love between dogs and foxes.

Me: I didn't know that.

Fox: Yeah, they bug me.

Me: Do you bug dogs?

Fox: Every chance I get!

Me: I mean do dogs dislike foxes?

Fox: I knew what you meant, I was just being foxy. Fact is, dogs are jealous of us.

Me: Why is that?

Fox: What do you mean?? Foxes are way better than dogs! Can a dog skulk?! I'm a great skulker! Every fox I know is. And dogs aren't even wild animals.

Me: Is that a big deal?

Fox: Are you drunk?! In the animal kingdom it's like the difference between an officer and an enlisted person! We kill for a living. Dogs get their dinner served up dead in a bowl. It makes them torpid. Why do you think the dog is lazy? Foxes can't afford the luxury of torpidity.

Me: So you were taunting the dog. I thought maybe you took a shortcut.

Fox: Are you delirious?! I went out of my way to jump that dog! I'll tell you what it is about dogs. They have the same genealogical roots as a fox but they never invite us in! If a dog's owner is away for the weekend and the neighbor is watching it—that's another thing: does a fox have to be watched? What am I, a pot of water?—if the dog is alone for the weekend would it kill the lethargic lump to invite me in through the doggy door? I would love to sit on a couch! It looks so comfortable. And would it hurt to share some kibble? Guess what a mouse tastes like? Exactly like you think it does!

Me (checks watch): Well... nice meeting you.

Fox: I'm sorry, am I keeping you?

Me: No, it's been great! I just have to... be somewhere.

Fox: But you don't want to say where.

Me: I have to go home and feed the dog.

The blazingly quick brown fox jumps over the dynamic human and skulks away.

New Curse Word

I wrote a song. It might also be a poem, but songs are more lucrative so it's a song.

It's time to get a new curse word,
the old ones are all worn out
I hear them wherever I go now
so they've mostly lost their clout

I decided to make a new one
I went off on a wordy binge
This is what I came up with
I hope one makes you cringe

First I thought of "grap,"
then I came up with "pring"
I tested out "tranker"
but they don't really sing

Then I invented "prake"
and took a shot with "radisser"
I got a little desperate
and let loose with "fugimmster!"

But I never found a good one
none had any zip
they didn't sound too dirty
like I was giving you some lip

I tried again for a winner
the muther foofer of 'em all
the one word I couldn't utter
near your family in a mall

I gave a shot to "flinker"
then called a guy a "poot"
I thought about "besuddler"
but didn't give a hoot

I don't think this is working
I think you're not offended
I just can't get a word out
that's disgusting yet also splendid

Nothing really worked for me
nothing ever stuck
I guess there's just no substitute
for a good old-fashioned fluck

If A Bear Attacks Play Dead?

Recently I read an article with advice that struck me as being hard to follow: if attacked by a mountain lion fight back, but if attacked by a bear play dead.

I have no problem with the mountain lion advice—I'll fight that lion, just as soon as I read an article on how to do it—but following the bear advice doesn't seem so easy.

If a newborn bear comes at me I'll be able to play dead, but a brand-new bruin is the size of your smallest finger and I'm not that threatened by your pinky. But a large bear, or a medium bear, or a scrawny bear in a bad mood and suddenly my life depends on something I don't think I have: acting ability! I once tried out for the role of "tree" in a school play and they said I would be better as a shrub. I was humiliated but said okay, I'll be a shrub, and they said the play had no shrub, it was just acting advice.

Intellectually I understand not running from a bear. The average bear, if it stayed within its lane and had qualified for the meet, would easily win the Olympic 100-meter dash. Bears run the hundred in about seven seconds. Usain Bolt's human record is 9.58. (Realistically, the bear would probably attack you right at the starting line, but the point is a bear is faster than you are, no matter who you are.)

If I can't outrun a bellicose bear and I'm no thespian, are there any other options? Some suggest climbing a tree. But with strength, claws and a reason—wanting to eat me—it seems like a bear could get up a tree better than I can. And why have I heard the phrase "treeing a bear"? I don't like the sound of it.

If I can't act, run or climb, that leaves fight. If a bear attacks and I have a gun I'll shoot, but I probably won't have a gun. How about a stick? Seems like a handy weapon on a forest floor.

So it's a stick and me against a bear. Do I hope to kill that bear? Hell yes I do! It started it! I not only want that bear dead, I'll sell its gallbladder to an impotent foreigner.

I realize I probably can't kill a bear with a stick, but maybe I can ward it off. I like those chances a lot better than staying in character while a 1,200-pound death machine sticks its nose on my face for a long wet sniff!

So if a bear much larger than your digitus minimus manus attacks, I will attempt to fight it off with the stick I now carry wherever I go.

Dietary Restrictions

Unless you're against eating all animals, other than cultural custom there's nothing inherently different from eating a chicken, a dog or a fish.

Some say the fish has less feelings so it's not as bad. But how do they know? To the fish I bet she or he has a lot of feelings. Feelings like don't eat me! The fish is penalized because of its lack of personality. To us. Maybe to trout certain trout are hilarious.

Same with a chicken. We eat it because its face isn't compelling, so we don't connect with it. Can you tell if a chicken is happy? I can't.

A dog is a friendly-faced animal so some cultures identify with it more, but what's the difference between a dog and a cow? One is way better with frisbees and the other can't climb on your lap, that's about it.

Guns For God

A few years ago Kentucky made it legal for priests to carry concealed weapons.

Good thing too, because soon after there was an incident in Bucky's Priest Supply.

Bucky is near the cash register counting communion wafers. Behind and around him are shelves full of prayer books, chalices, shotguns, robes, pistols, mitres, rifles, offering plates, ammo and a floor full of pews.

BUCKY (counting out wafers): ...vi, vii, viii—

The chime on the door tinkles as Father Reload, one of the toughest priests in Kentucky, enters. The Father wears a long priestly robe.

BUCKY: Mornin' father, how do?

FATHER RELOAD: Morning, Bucky. Are those the new gluten-free wafers?

BUCKY: Yes indeedy, nothing but natural for this holy host! Hey, we got some nice baptismal fonts in. Guaranteed to save 5,000 souls!

FATHER RELOAD: No thanks, but I could use a dashboard Jesus.

BUCKY: With or without stigmata?

FATHER RELOAD: With. Always.

BUCKY (reaching for a box): Stigmata it is...

FATHER RELOAD: And I'll need a couple of pipes for our organ—a high c and an f sharp, please—plus a case of those "Expect a Miracle" bumperstickers.

BUCKY: Can I interest you in a dribble chalice?

FATHER RELOAD: Funny, Bucky, but not today. I'll take the dashboard Jesus with me, please send the rest to the church.

BUCKY: You got it, Father.

FATHER RELOAD: Bless you, Bucky.

The Father does the sign of the cross, pockets the dashboard Jesus and heads for the door.

BUCKY: You know we're sellin' guns now, Father. Can I show you something in a Luger?

The Priest hikes up his robe to reveal two pistols strapped to a thigh.

FATHER RELOAD: I think I'm good.

BUCKY: That's a nice arsenal, Father, but unless you got more firepower hidden in there you are bereft of automatic weaponry.

FATHER RELOAD: Well, I keep two in my apse.

BUCKY: As you should. You good for grenades?

FATHER RELOAD: Gave 'em up for Lent.

BUCKY (hopeful): We got some St. Christopher bazookas in…

FATHER RELOAD: Maybe for a Methodist, but we Catholics are meek.

BUCKY: Except the Kennedys!

FATHER RELOAD: Touché, Bucky. Thanks for everything. A hearty hallelujah to you and the missus!

BUCKY: Right back at ya, Padre… well, not the missus part.

The Father is near the door when three Catholic high school girls enter dressed in school uniforms. They're seniors and they're cocky. They pretend to innocently shop but they're up to something as they exchange a series of secret winks and nods.

Suddenly the leader of the schoolgirls gropes beneath her skirt and pulls out a pink pistol.

SCHOOLGIRL LEADER: Freeze, Padre! You too, Hillbilly Elegy!

The other two girls pull out stylishly colorful guns and take up positions designed to show they mean business.

SCHOOLGIRL LEADER: This is a stickup! We want all the school uniforms. We're sick of this boring junk so we're going to burn it all and wear leggings and bustiers!

SCHOOLGIRL (to Bucky): Hand over the white cotton blouses, now!

OTHER SCHOOLGIRL: And the cardigans, mister! Do it!

As Bucky grabs the garments Father Reload pulls out a pistol and fires a warning shot into a stack of choir robes.

FATHER RELOAD: That's enough, girls! Put down the navy blue blazers! Now!

It's tense until the Schoolgirl Leader finally relents.

SCHOOLGIRL LEADER: Okay, girls, drop the weapons. And the knee-high socks. We're sorry, Father, repentant even. This wool is just so itchy and unattractive.

FATHER RELOAD: I understand, but it's the way of God. Please my children, kneel.

As the girls recite the Rosary, Bucky tosses the Father an assault pistol in a holster, which he straps to a thigh as he heads for the door.

The chime tinkles.

Screen Speeches
That Ended up on
The Cutting Room Floor

I purchased the contents of a foreclosed storage unit recently, and among the items I found in the unit was an old reel of film. I hired a projectionist to screen the film and it turned out to be deleted scenes from three classic movies and an old tv show. For the sake of screen scholarship I transcribed the dialogue.

<u>Tony Montana, *Scarface* (to Manny's corpse)</u>: "Manny, I so sorry I killed you! But why didn't you invite me to your wedding?? Then I woulda known you wasn't just secretly plowing my sister, you loved each other. Try to see it from my zapatos: I tell you to stay away from my

sister, then I go to her house and find you both wearing loose bathrobes and sweaty smiles, so I shot you. How could I know your intentions were good?! If you didn't invite me to your wedding because I might've killed you I understand, but you coulda called from the chapel when it was over! I hear weird music in my head when my sister is around but I mighta been able to accept the marriage. In a few years. Then I woulda given you the best wedding presents: a toaster oven and a tiger!"

Frodo, *Lord of the Rings*: "Bilbo, I know I've been acting oddly lately, beyond all the ring stuff. I have a confession. It's a shocker. I'm involved in forbidden love! I'm engaged to an Orc! I know they're our sworn enemy but this one is so bewitching. I love how her ears stick out straight to the side. Huge turn-on. Sometimes I wish she were a little less mutilated, maybe throw on some moisturizer, but she's committed to being herself and I respect the full package. Just don't let her bite you! But how do I tell my mother??"

Henry Hill, *Goodfellas*: "Yes, Tommy, I think you're funny. Not necessarily like a clown, but you amuse me. It's not just me. You amuse everyone. So I said you're funny? So what. I never said you're so ugly platypuses wince. I never said I'd be making love to your mother right now except she has the football team over on

Tuesdays. Or that your favorite appendage is so small you need tweezers to urinate. Which is close to the truth. I just meant you have a rollicking evocative delivery full of mirthful bonhomie. Now where's Spider, I need a drink? Oh, right. We need to hire someone."

Gilligan, *Gilligan's Island*: "Skipper, do you know my last name? Do you even know I have one?? I don't think you care about me other than as a whipping boy for your stupid hat! By the way, have you ever thought about how much money you owe me? I was hired for a three-hour tour. At $1.30 an hour since you only pay minimum wage! And is the tour over? No! I admit we've had some close calls in which some might say I was the main reason we didn't return to civilization, but this isn't the first time you hired me—you knew my peccadilloes! And it's only $1.30 for the first eight hours. After that it's time-and-a-half. That's $1.95 an hour times 15 years! And why do I always get the bottom bunk? Why can't I tie my hammock to those two posts over there and have my own area? Every night I fall asleep with the fear that a large man who owes me a lot of money "forgot" to tie his hammock right. By the way, my last name is Winklemeyer—and don't ever use it!"

I Don't like Killing Frogs

Who dislikes a frog?

A toad maybe, but it's probably out of envy and if you envy something you must like it.

The point is, you can probably understand not liking to kill frogs, especially accidentally. (Either way, really.)

But if you've lived in the upper East of the U.S. you know that after it rains, in the early evening of a warm summer day frogs like to sit in the road.

Or maybe to a frog it's standing.

When I'm driving in these conditions, every few minutes a frog is in my way or one jumps in front of me.

I concentrate hard to avoid them and I'm not aware of any that I've hit, but in three years of living here have I missed every single one?

Should I just not drive in these situations? That seems impractical. Should I concentrate harder to avoid them? That seems unsafe. I might hit something I'd miss even more.

Or should I blithely cruise along and write it off as nature's way of ridding the gene pool of creatures who should know better by now? If a frog can recognize the threat of a bigmouth bass, why not a radial tire?

Wait! Maybe that's it. Maybe all it takes is tying a bigmouth bass to the front of my car! I'll give it a try.

I hope it works because I love frogs. I don't want them to croak.

IF A TREE FALLS IN THE FOREST

People sometimes ask, "If a tree falls in the forest but no one hears it, does it still make a sound?"

If you are one of these people perplexed by this puzzler I do not mean to shock you, but yes, it still makes a sound. Falling trees do not possess the ability to detect if humans are around and if none are to suppress their heft. Trees are not that talented.

To hopefully clear it up once and for all: when a tree falls it makes a sound, usually a big sound. Unless it's a small tree, then it makes a smaller sound. But sound is involved. This principle applies to almost every falling object.

If you look into it, and I did right before starting this sentence, many people say "Sound only occurs if there's vibration on the tympanic membrane, aka the eardrum. No membrane, no sound."

That actually makes sense. My bad.

A "Bro" Breaks Up

I know things have been tense between us, and I think you're worried it's because we're getting married in two days and can't take anything back without losing not only the deposit but in many cases full payment for things like every item your father is covering.

And you're right, it is because we're getting married in two days. And I know it's late to bring this up, but I don't want to be married. Marriage maybe, probably, but not this one. I feel like a bristlecone pine already, bent over by four thousand years of high-altitude wind.

You said you were sensing a distance between us. That was last year in grad school, which I mention because I never told you you were correct. I meant to, then the waitress came over. So there has been a distance between us, and I don't mean to be mean but I'd like to add more distance.

I know at time like this a person in my shoes has a lot to answer for. But let's not forget that the whole reason for an engagement is to give couples a chance to ramp up into marriage, or provide the knowledge that gravity is against them and they're not gonna make it up that incline. We are living embodiers of this profound wisdom of the ages! Except the part about your dad having to pay $124,000 for the hotel's platinum package.

(Can you believe "embodiers" is really a word? I would've used it anyway!)

Ex-future dad, I realize that a person in your shoes would be upset that a person in my shoes (sounds like we both lost our shoes!) would cause him to lose $144,000, plus flowers, photographer, videographer, booze, lutist, flutist, rose petals, church, minister, organist and 16 non-refundable premium coach seats with 35" legroom. But it wasn't wasted because I learned so much about not wanting to marry your daughter! The system worked. Booyah.

Now that I'm attuning to all this, I would say I suspected the first time in high school when we interacted on the tobacco-juiced floor of the visitor's dugout that I didn't think we'd stay together forever, but I couldn't break up with her. She was good at my homework and nifty in the dugout, what can I say.

You know what, I'll send you a check.

Severe Tire Damage

A lonely parking lot is surrounded by chain-link fence. There are bushes by an entrance.

A man enters and finds his car easily. It's the only one in the lot. The man gets in his car and drives to the nearest exit, but a sturdy chain blocks the way. He looks for another way out. The only other opening is by the bushes.

The man drives to the other opening but stops when he sees a sign that says "No Exit. Severe Tire Damage." The frustrated man honks his horn, but no one hears him, at least no one responds.

Then the man notices there are no metal teeth in the pavement to puncture his tires. He hops out to confirm the absence of a threat.

The man gets back in his car and starts to drive out of the lot, but as his front bumper edges to freedom four hooded ninjas with machetes leap from the bushes to slash his tires! The ninjas shred his tires in a brief but expert frenzy then disappear back in the bushes.

The terrified man looks around, then screams when the ninjas return with machine guns to blast his tires! The ninjas keep firing until they run out of bullets then vanish as quickly as they came.

The stunned man cowers at the wheel. Despite the wildness of the attack the only damage is to the tires. Even the rims are unscathed. The man looks around in shock but doesn't see anyone. He quickly exits the car and tries to run but he's so shaken he mostly wobbles.

As the man hurries away, unseen by him a lone ninja springs from the bushes, forces open the car's trunk, removes the spare tire, sets it on the ground, puts a grenade under it and disappears back in the shrubbery. The tire explodes!

Hey, the man was warned.

YOU CAN KEEP
THE OLD WEST

Regarding the Old West, I've noticed many people romanticize how life was back then: the aura, the myth, the feeling. I don't miss the Old West one bit.

To me the main feature of the Old West, other than death, danger and guns, was an almost total lack of personal cleanliness.

You might surmise that the Old West was no dirtier or perhaps even less dirty than most or all previous eras, and your point might be that if people have been dirty through the ages then the Old West would get the nod over any other era, and maybe even today's era. But my point (we may not get back to you having a point again) is isn't *now* the best time? Aren't the medical advances, high literacy rates and ever-shrinking bikinis a lot better than a dentist with whiskey and a pair of pliers?

Other stuff bugs me about the Old West too. For instance the people who were there before us. I'm uneasy trespassing on the land of people who have good reason to mistrust me and carry arrows. Forget whether they have guns, right at the news of arrows I quiver.

The gunslinger factor is also a big worry. A lot of people had guns back then. A lot of people shoot pool today and I'm about average at pool, so if everyone had a gun and I practiced occasionally like I do with pool there would still be big bevies of people who could outdraw me, and if life is mainly about guns and I'm only so-so as a shooter what's so great about that?

One of my biggest barriers to liking the Old West is cows. Evidently most people were cowboys back then, but why are we so captivated by people who work with cows, then and today? Cows are okay to eat if no turkeys are available, but I wouldn't want to spend all day with them. Who wants to ride on a horse in the heat to rope a dogie when you can ride in a car with air conditioning to get a steak? Both times I'm sitting on leather in pursuit of beef, I'd rather be enclosed. If I want fresh air I'll open a window.

That's just the big stuff. There's a lot of small stuff I wouldn't like about the Old West. Disease. Amputation. An almost complete lack of ointments.

Let's say you're traveling. Where does the stagecoach stop to go to the loo? Behind a cactus. What are the details after that? Doesn't matter, count me out.

And I haven't dug into the statistics, but I'll bet there was quite a bit of food poisoning back then. If you don't know enough to sanitize before a caesarian what are the chances you can tell if a turkey has turned?

I do look good in a vest, but I'm not convinced it was better or even good back then. How can you be happy if you smell worse than your horse?

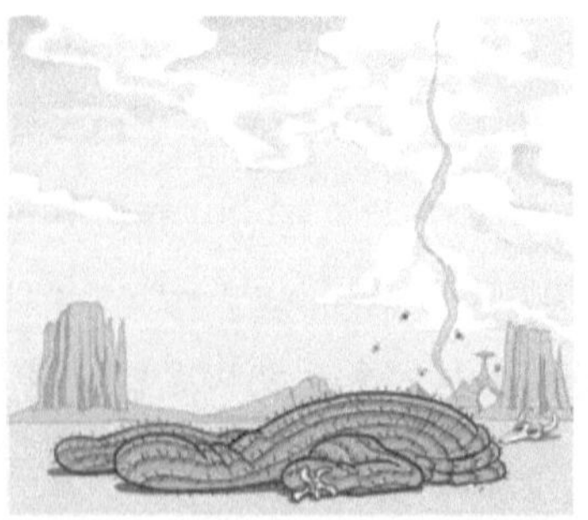

THE SECRET LIFE OF
BOB MITTY

"The Secret Life of Walter Mitty" is a very famous, very short story (under six pages) by legendary American humorist James Thurber.

Walter Mitty, the timorous henpecked husband of a dauntingly domineering woman, frequently slips into daydreams to avoid his hectoring wife and humdrum life.

Unlike in his real life, in his secret life Walter Mitty is heroic. He's a brave Navy commander in a terrible storm, a famous heart surgeon called in for an impossible operation, a cocksure defendant who acts honorably to a beleaguered woman in court, and a combat pilot gutsy enough to fly a plane by himself even though it takes two people to fly it.

Each time he's off in a heroic reverie, Mitty is brought back to reality by his wife or sometimes a stranger asking him to do something or not do something or drive slower or drive faster. At one point he gets criticized by his wife for not being noticeable sitting in a hotel lobby chair.

Even if we've never been henpecked by a spouse, most of us have daydreamed about being a person of action. I've never daydreamed about being a person of action because I already am one, but a lot of other people have.

I'm more prone to imagining things that could go wrong. For me it's like if Walter Mitty had a brother, Bob Mitty.

In "The Secret Life of Bob Mitty," Bob daydreams about falling boulders, rogue waves, societal collapse, partial societal collapse, debris flow, impending societal collapse, the amount of privately-owned tigers in the U.S. (over 5,000), being ticketed for littering if a napkin blows out of his car, a bug flying up his nose and eventually dying there (but only after a frantic hour in the woods trying to extract it, then a three-hour drive—for two of which the bug is still alive—to an urgicenter to remove a moth that got shoved up there much farther than necessary by repeated panicked pokes of a sap-laden twig).

These fears aren't based on nothing. I was once in a convenience store and a police officer with a gun in a holster was in line ahead of me, and a person entered the store pushing a bicycle and tripped and fell and the bike almost hit me, and I imagined the bike knocking me into the police officer and my hand innocently landing on the officer's gun and accidentally unsnapping the strap on the holster and the officer thinking it was on purpose and justifiably killing me. People are almost killed like that every day. That's "The Secret Life of Bob Mitty."

Do you ever worry that while driving at night you'll signal for a lane change and accidentally flash your brights, and the car ahead of you will be filled with disgruntled stabbers and they'll trap your car and stab you just because your brights switch is too touchy? Bob has.

Bob imagines he'll be in a restaurant and say "Do you have any coffee, uh—" but two booths away they thought he said "Do you have any mafia?" and the people two booths away are in the mafia and they think Bob is an informant so they shoot him seven times.

Walter Mitty imagines himself as a heroic doctor. Bob Mitty imagines discovering mold in his cheese spread, but only after eating six cracker-loads of the stuff.

Sure it's fun to escape a termagant wife by fantasizing about being a brave captain in a raging storm, but Bob and I are more inclined to daydream about... being bitten by a brown recluse spider... going to a job interview and thinking you nailed it, then on the drive home noticing in the rearview mirror you have cheetos in your teeth... waving to someone in your car, and the person in the car next to you thinks you gave them the finger, and the person is another disgruntled stabber who traps your car, and you and your passengers get stabbed... getting caught under a huge flock of seagulls... which happened to me once, though I was able to run away from most of their flight path and somehow remain unsoiled... greeting the president at a public event after you just ate spoiled sushi and it was really spoiled so you get no warning before you throw up all over the president and get arrested for assault, but the judge knows the president socially and unethically delays the arraignment so you're jailed for two weeks without bail and guess what? There are disgruntled stabbers in jail and they keep trying to stab you... wolves..

In the last 20 years or so a change has occurred to tv remote controls. Before that if you were on mute and hit volume the sound would unmute. Now you have to push volume twice to unmute.

Pushing a button an extra time doesn't add convenience, so the remote control people added it because... they were worried I might accidentally unmute? Is that really a danger I need to be protected from?

What was that meeting like at the remote control factory?

"...and if a person puts it on mute, we're making it so they can turn the sound back on with either the mute button or the volume button?"

"Yeah, pretty standard."

"Now the green button! We deserve to be heard!"

"Then the yellow button! We deserve to be heard too!"

"Same with us!" shouts the blue button team. "Everybody worships the red button."

The red button team sits back smugly. "You can debate your little functions all day, but when it comes to life and death everyone answers to the power button."

"No!" yells the pause button team leader. "The power button is no more than the keys to the car! The car is all the other buttons. The channel buttons are huge! And what about menu?! On and off is merely a gatekeeper, a nightwatchman!"

"We'll get to the other buttons! Right now we're talking about volume. I have an idea for coming out of mute. Say the tv is on mute and the viewer presses volume and the sound comes back on. Great if it was intentional, but what if it was an accidental unmute? How do we know?! I think we've been cavalier not to verify their wishes once they go off-button. We have a societal responsibility here! How about coming out of mute you have to push volume twice to unmute? Without a verification step I think we leave ourselves wide open legally, not to mention morally and sonically!"

"Omigosh! There could be serious consequences from an accidental unmute. Say a spouse is sleeping and an accidental unmute occurs and the spouse wakes up. But what if the spouse can't get back to sleep for several hours? Now in the morning they're tired so on the way to work they cause a fiery crash with a lot of death and quite a bit of dismemberment. Having viewers push volume twice will save lives! And limbs."

"Or someone could accidentally unmute when a burglar is in the house and the burglar panics and strangles the entire family and two of their three houseguests."

"We might as well have strangled them ourselves!"

"Okay, from now on it takes two pushes of the volume button to unmute. This is a landmark day in handset history! We just added a chapter to the book of human wisdom! I feel like Oppenheimer guiding his team. Okay, moving on, now what's all this talk about changing the square buttons to round?!"

the LAZY DOG

I ran into the quick brown fox again. We got to talking and I said I wanted to see the lazy dog it jumped over.

The fox seemed a little put out that, just like on page 60, I wanted to leave to see a pet, so the irked brown fox told me the address then jumped over me and skulked away. Again!

When I got to the house it wasn't hard to find the lazy dog. The lassitudinous lump was spread out like a jellyfish on one side of a wraparound porch.

As I stood on the sidewalk wondering what the lazy dog would say about the quick brown fox if it could speak, the dog shockingly spoke.

<u>Dog</u>: Can I help you?

<u>Me</u>: You can talk?!

<u>Dog</u>: Either that or I'm animatronic. Why are you staring at me?

<u>Me</u>: I met the fox who jumped over you, the quick brown one, and I was curious about you. The fox can talk too! What a coincidence! Did you know the fox can talk?

<u>Dog</u>: Yeah, it won't shut up.

<u>Me</u>: It's great to meet you. You're pretty famous.

<u>Dog</u>: Famous for being jumped over? Big honor. Thanks so much.

<u>Me</u>: At least you can talk. How did you learn?

<u>Dog</u>: The fox kept jumping over me so I moved here where—

<u>Me</u>: The fox jumped over you more than once?!

<u>Dog</u>: Don't remind me. It was a humiliating period.

<u>Me</u>: Sounds like the jumping has stopped.

<u>Dog</u>: When I moved over here by the window the fox couldn't get enough running room to clear me so the jumping stopped. But I can't shake the feeling that the fox is still eyeing me, hoping to jump over me again. It haunts me. Do you hear that?

<u>Me</u>: I just hear the tv through the window. Sounds like *Days of Our Lives*.

<u>Dog</u>: Very good. That's how I learned to talk. I can't believe Kyle is leaving Summer!

<u>Me</u>: So sad. Did you ever say anything to the quick brown fox as it jumped over you?

<u>Dog</u>: I didn't want to give it the satisfaction so I pretended the jumps didn't bother me. But when I moved over here it probably knew.

<u>Me</u>: Why do you think the fox kept jumping over you?

<u>Dog</u>: It's hard to jump under someone.

<u>Me</u>: I meant—

<u>Dog</u>: Fact is, foxes are jealous of us.

<u>Me</u>: Why is that?

<u>Dog</u>: What do you mean?! Dogs are way better than foxes! Dogs live indoors and foxes sleep in a hole. Case closed! The quick brown fox always wants to eat my food and sit on the couch. That's not foxlike. Be yourself, fox! Foxes are a risk for rabies and my humans have a litter of three. We can't chill.

<u>Me</u>: Does it bother you that everyone says you're lazy?

<u>Dog</u>: I've made peace with gravity. It's relentless. What's wrong with sitting around all day? I'm a dog. What should I do, take up crafting? I'm not lazy, I just can't grip a glue gun!

<u>Me</u>: I'm guessing you don't like to play fetch.

Dog: I don't like any object enough to get it forty times, let alone a stick. Who cares about a stick? Same with a ball. If you throw it across a lawn I'll get it. Once. To chew on. But I'm not bringing it back just to go get it again. Why do dogs who play fetch even need a stick? They can run back and forth by themselves. Be your own stick!

Me: Why not let the fox inside once in a while? Just curious.

Dog: I'm bathed and groomed regularly. Foxes smell like wet wool bathed in urine and musk. I'd rather be indoors with a flatulent beaver.

Me: Copy that. The fox said if animals were in the military wild animals would be officers and pets would be soldiers.

Dog: Obviously the fox gave you that "We kill for a living" speech. If live food is so great why does the fox covet my kibble? If living in a den is so delightful why does the fox want to sit on my sofa?

The lazy dog stops talking. It listens intently (as intently as a lazy dog can). All I hear is Marlena and John arguing from the tv, as they've been doing for 37 years.

The lazy dog perks up. An ear anyway, which is a lot for the dog.

The dog and I hear something in the bushes by the porch. I'm scared and the dog is frightened.

The lazy dog starts to get up. Twenty seconds later it's standing. The dog and I creep fearfully to the edge of the porch to look down when a quick brown flash jumps over us and skulks away. Again!

"Like sands through the hourglass, these are the days of our lives..."

Disappointing Geographical Nomenclature
Part Two

As a follow-up to the thing about the naming of K-2, I decided to visit Mt. K-2 in person. I'd already researched it extensively for close to an hour so I was heavily invested and had to go.

The thing no one tells you about mountains is that they can talk. Or was I just oxygen-deprived?

All I know is I was standing there, alone in my crampons because my guide had left to scout ahead, when I heard a voice.

Voice: Hey buddy, how you doing? Pretty cold up here, huh?

Me (confused): Tenzing...?

Tenzing is my guide and a great-grandson of the famous Sherpa guide Tenzing Norgay, who climbed Mt. Everest with Edmund Hillary on the first ascent.

Voice: It's not Tenzing. It's me, the mountain.

Me: That's amazing! I've met a talking fox and a talking dog but never a mountain.

Voice (K-2): Today is my first day of talking! I'm young for a mountain. I turn 65 million on Wednesday. I've seen a lot of people, though none before 1856, and I've understood them for decades, but this morning I finally spoke! Talking is fun. You look cold. I can't help it, it's my nature. Though it's been getting warmer lately.

Me: Great to meet you, K-2. I have a few questions.

K-2 (confused): Who are you talking to?

Me: You.

K-2: Who's K-2??

Me: You are. Anyway, just a couple of questions.

K-2: Can we go back to conversational base camp?

Me: Sure, but I don't know what that means.

K-2: You said my name is K-2. Are you serious?! That's a terrible name!

<u>Me</u>: I wouldn't call it mellifluous, but you have personality.

<u>K-2</u>: Thanks, but what happened? How did I get that name??

<u>Me</u>: It's supposed to be a temporary name until the local name is determined.

<u>K-2</u>: How long until they find the local name?!

<u>Me</u>: It's been 168 years so it's not looking good.

<u>K-2</u> (crying): They didn't name me? They don't like me??

<u>Me</u>: It's not that! They couldn't see you.

<u>K-2</u>: That's not so bad. Sorry about the crying. I'm young, it happens. I hope none of the other mountains heard me.

<u>Me</u>: All mountains can hear?

<u>K-2</u>: And talk. And these mountains already told me they don't like me! The first day I learn to talk and my neighbors tell me I'm too tall and I intimidate them. There are some pretty insecure mountains around here! I hope they heard that.

<u>Me</u>: You are the second tallest mountain in the world.

<u>K-2</u>: Second tallest?? Wow! I had no idea. How many mountains are there? Seven, eight thousand...?

<u>Me</u>: 1,187,049.

<u>K-2</u> (thrilled): Seriously?!? Over a million mountains look up to me?

<u>Me</u>: All but one.

<u>K-2</u>: I've always wondered where I rank. Awful name, though. Depressing. How do I change it?

<u>Me</u>: I'm actually starting a movement to rename you! I mean name you. A temporary name is not a name as far as I'm concerned.

<u>K-2</u>: That is so kind of you! Thanks for doing that.

<u>Me</u>: You deserve it.

<u>K-2</u>: I've always liked the name Gary.

<u>Me</u>: Maybe don't rush into anything.

History Unhidden II
More Little-Known Facts About Historical Figures

Orville and Wilbur Wright would've flown five years earlier had it not been for their other brother, Fredo Wright.

The Pied Piper of Hamelin was actually from Bückeburg, two towns over.

Andy Warhol was paid by Campbell's soup all along.

Lawrence of Arabia had a vacation home in Chad.

George Orwell's *Animal Farm* was originally titled *Cropland of Chordates.*

Attila the Hun was dyslexic, but he was illiterate so it didn't matter.

Vermeer's first title for his most famous painting was *The Girl With No Pearl Earring*, then his art dealer had a suggestion.

German philosopher Johann Goethe wrote "To witness two lovers is a spectacle for the gods." He was later arrested for peeking in his neighbors' window.

In third grade Alexander the Great led an assault against the fourth grade and enslaved them.

Rembrandt painted more than 40 self-portraits, but forensic evidence reveals they're all of his neighbor, Frans.

If Karl Marx doesn't have a bad experience with his childhood lemonade stand history turns out differently.

Moses only parted the Red Sea because ever since the basket thing he had a paralyzing fear of boats. And rattan.

The End.

About the Author

McNickle has always loved comedy, which isn't necessarily a good sign.

He enjoys short walks on the beach, likes boats if there's no land around and wishes he had started reading Emerson sooner.

Recently, as in while writing this page, McNickle discovered he enjoys talking about himself in the third person.

Is there a fourth person, he wondered? Turns out there is. Example: 'One is led to understand...'

Is there a fifth person? Not yet, but McNickle is working on it.

Future Books by McNickle

"Nudity, Yeah!'

"A Tale of Twelve Cities." Dickens did great but this has ten more cities! Don't worry, the book will have a guillotine.

"I Was Kidnapped by Aliens, but They Were Chill and Apologized For Misreading My Answer When They Asked If I Wanted To Go With Them and Thought I Said Yes"

"My Weekends With Supermodels: Do's and Don'ts"

"How to Stop Reading Self-Help Books"

"McNickle Marries: A Real-Life Look at the Fairy-Tale Wedding to His Legendary Soulmate"

"Nudity, Oh Yeah!" Sequel to beloved first book.

Appreciation

Thank you for reading this.

Not just that sentence, all the ones before it too.

love,
McNickle